Interferometer Ethics

Measuring Moral Wavelengths

Raymond Mcdaniel

Chapter 1: Ethical Frameworks as Interferometers

The Nature of Light and the Nature of Morality

Light, in all its ethereal splendor, has captivated humanity for millennia. We've harnessed its power, studied its properties, and marveled at its ability to illuminate the world around us. Yet, light also holds a curious duality. It behaves as both a wave and a particle, a paradox that challenges our very understanding of the physical world. Morality, too, possesses a similar enigmatic nature. It guides our actions, shapes our societies, and provides a framework for what we deem right and wrong. But like light, its essence remains elusive, a concept that seems both concrete and intangible, absolute and relative, all at once. Perhaps, then, it's not so far-fetched to consider the nature of light as a metaphor for understanding the very nature of morality itself.

Just as light travels in waves, morality seems to ebb and flow through history. What was once considered morally acceptable – slavery, for instance – can become morally reprehensible as our collective understanding evolves. These shifts, like the peaks and troughs of a light wave, demonstrate the dynamic and ever-changing nature of ethical frameworks. Yet, just as light also exhibits particle-like behavior, morality, too, can feel absolute and unwavering. Certain core principles, like the inherent value of human life or the importance of truth-telling, seem to resonate deeply within us, acting as fundamental moral "particles" that underpin our ethical decision-making.

Consider the concept of consequentialism, an ethical framework that judges the morality of an action based on its outcomes. Like measuring the brightness of light, consequentialists focus on the intensity of the consequences. The "brighter" the outcome – the more happiness or well-being it produces – the more morally right the action is deemed to be. Conversely, actions that lead to "dimmer" outcomes, those filled with suffering or harm, are judged as morally wrong. This approach, however, can lead to complex dilemmas. How do we accurately predict all potential consequences, both immediate and far-reaching? What if achieving a "brighter" outcome for some necessitates a "dimmer" outcome for others?

Deontology, in contrast, operates on a fixed spectrum of duty and obligation. Like the unwavering lines of a spectrograph, deontological principles provide a clear and defined framework for ethical behavior. Actions are judged as inherently right or wrong based on their adherence to these pre-established rules, regardless of their potential consequences. Telling the truth, for example, is considered a moral duty in many deontological systems, even if it might lead to unfavorable outcomes in certain situations. This emphasis on unwavering principles provides a sense of moral clarity and consistency. However, it can also lead to rigid interpretations that struggle to accommodate the nuances of complex ethical dilemmas.

Virtue ethics, on the other hand, focuses on cultivating moral character and striving for ethical excellence. Imagine a beam of light passing through a polarizing filter. Only light waves oscillating in a particular direction can pass through, creating a beam of enhanced coherence and intensity. Similarly, virtue ethics encourages individuals to cultivate inner virtues – compassion, honesty, courage – that align with their moral compass. By strengthening these moral "filters," individuals can refine their actions and judgments, striving towards a life characterized by ethical coherence and moral integrity.

Just as the study of light requires us to grapple with its paradoxical nature, understanding morality demands that we embrace its complexities. It is a tapestry woven from the threads of consequence, duty, and character, constantly interacting and influencing one another. By viewing morality through the lens of light, we gain a deeper appreciation for its multifaceted nature, its capacity for both change and constancy, and its profound power to illuminate the path towards a more ethical and just world.

Consequentialism Measuring the Brightness of Outcomes

Imagine a world where every moral decision boiled down to a simple equation: maximize happiness, minimize suffering. This, in essence, is the core tenet of consequentialism, an ethical framework that judges the morality of an action solely by its outcomes. Like a beacon cutting through the darkness, consequentialism illuminates a path towards a brighter future, one where actions are evaluated based on their ability to generate the greatest good for the greatest number.

At the heart of this approach lies the principle of utility, a measure of the overall happiness or well-being generated by an action. Think of it as measuring the "brightness" of an outcome. Actions that produce a surplus of happiness – a radiant burst of light – are deemed morally right, while those that result in suffering cast a shadow of moral wrongness. This emphasis on maximizing positive outcomes has a certain intuitive appeal. After all, isn't the goal of morality to create a better world for everyone?

Consider the classic example of a runaway trolley barreling towards five unsuspecting individuals. You have the opportunity to pull a lever, diverting the trolley onto a side track where it will strike only one person. A consequentialist, faced with this dilemma, would likely advocate for pulling the lever. Saving five lives at the cost of one, they would argue, produces a net positive outcome, a brighter overall result despite the tragic loss. This focus on maximizing happiness, even in the face of difficult choices, underscores the pragmatic nature of consequentialism.

However, this seemingly straightforward approach to morality is not without its complexities. One of the most significant challenges lies in accurately predicting and measuring the consequences of our actions. Life is rarely a simple equation, and actions often ripple outward, creating unforeseen consequences that can be difficult to anticipate. How can we be certain that an action intended to produce a positive outcome won't inadvertently lead to unintended negative consequences down the line?

Furthermore, consequentialism grapples with the question of whose happiness matters most. Should we prioritize the happiness of those closest to us – family, friends, fellow citizens – or strive for a more impartial calculus that considers the well-being of all sentient beings equally? And what about future generations? Should their potential happiness or suffering factor into our moral equations today?

These questions highlight the inherent difficulty of quantifying happiness and suffering, concepts that are often subjective and context-dependent. What brings joy to one person may cause pain to another, and what constitutes a "bright" outcome can vary widely across cultures and societies. This subjectivity raises concerns about the potential for bias and manipulation. Could consequentialism be used to justify actions that benefit a select few at the expense of others, all under the guise of maximizing overall happiness?

Despite these challenges, consequentialism offers a valuable framework for navigating the complexities of moral decision-making. It encourages us to think critically about the potential impact of our actions, to consider the well-being of all those affected, and to strive towards outcomes that promote happiness and alleviate suffering. By focusing on the consequences of our choices, we can illuminate a path towards a more ethical and compassionate world, one where the brightness of our collective future is measured by the well-being of all.

Deontology The Fixed Spectrum of Duty

Imagine a world governed by unwavering principles, where right and wrong are not subject to the shifting sands of consequence but etched in an unyielding moral code. This is the realm of deontology, an ethical framework that illuminates morality through the lens of duty and obligation. Like a prism separating light into its constituent colors, deontology reveals a fixed spectrum of moral rules, each representing a fundamental principle guiding ethical behavior.

At the heart of deontology lies the belief that certain actions are inherently right or wrong, regardless of their outcomes. Telling the truth, keeping promises, respecting the autonomy of others – these actions are not judged by their potential consequences but by their adherence to universal moral laws. These laws, often viewed as absolute and unchanging, provide a steadfast compass for navigating the often-turbulent waters of moral decision-making.

Consider the classic example of a person seeking refuge from imminent danger. They arrive at your doorstep, pleading for you to hide them from pursuers you know to be intent on harming them. Moments later, the pursuers arrive, demanding to know if you have seen the fugitive. A consequentialist might argue that lying is justified in this instance, as it would likely lead to the best outcome – protecting an innocent life. A deontologist, however, would likely maintain that lying is inherently wrong, a violation of a fundamental moral principle. Upholding the moral law, even in the face of potentially dire consequences, becomes paramount.

This unwavering commitment to principle is a defining characteristic of deontology. It provides a sense of moral clarity and consistency, a firm foundation upon which to build ethical frameworks. The Ten Commandments, with their clear-cut prohibitions against stealing, killing, and bearing false witness, exemplify this deontological approach. These rules are not open to interpretation or situational exceptions; they stand as immutable pillars of moral conduct.

However, this rigidity, while offering a sense of certainty, can also present challenges. Life is rarely black and white, and strict adherence to moral absolutes can sometimes lead to morally counterintuitive outcomes. What happens when two or more moral duties come into conflict, forcing us to choose between competing obligations?

Critics argue that deontology, in its strict adherence to rules, can sometimes fail to account for the nuances of complex ethical dilemmas. They point to situations where blindly following a rule might lead to more harm than good, highlighting the need for a more nuanced approach that considers the context in which moral decisions are made.

Furthermore, the question of who determines these universal moral laws remains a point of contention. Different cultures and societies may have varying interpretations of what constitutes right and wrong, leading to a diversity of ethical frameworks. This raises questions about the universality of deontological principles and the potential for cultural bias to influence the very rules that govern our moral behavior.

Despite these critiques, deontology offers a valuable perspective on the nature of morality. It emphasizes the importance of moral principles, the inherent value of duty and obligation, and the need for consistency in our ethical decision-making. By anchoring ourselves to a fixed spectrum of moral laws, we strive to create a world where actions are guided not by the shifting tides of consequence but by the enduring principles of right and wrong.

Virtue Ethics Cultivating Moral Coherence

Imagine morality not as a set of rules or a calculation of outcomes, but as a state of being, a way of living that emanates from within. This is the essence of virtue ethics, an ancient philosophy that emphasizes the cultivation of moral character above all else. Like a gardener tending to their plants, virtue ethicists believe that ethical behavior arises from nurturing virtuous traits – compassion, honesty, courage, wisdom – allowing these inner qualities to blossom and guide our actions.

Rather than focusing on what we "should do" in any given situation, virtue ethics asks: "What kind of person do I want to be?" It shifts the emphasis from external rules and consequences to the internal compass guiding our choices. Instead of adhering to a fixed moral code or calculating potential outcomes, we strive to embody virtues that align with our deepest values, allowing these qualities to shape our perceptions and guide our actions naturally.

Think of it like learning a musical instrument. A novice musician might meticulously follow sheet music, hitting each note with technical precision but lacking soul. A virtuous musician, however, embodies the music, allowing their internal sense of rhythm and melody to flow through them. Their actions, while still grounded in technique, become an expression of their inner musicality. Similarly, a virtuous person navigates the world with a moral fluency, their actions resonating with their deeply held values.

Central to virtue ethics is the concept of "eudaimonia," often translated as "flourishing" or "living well." It's not merely about fleeting happiness or pleasure, but a state of genuine fulfillment derived from living in accordance with one's virtues. Imagine a life where honesty flows effortlessly, where compassion guides your interactions, and courage empowers you to face challenges with integrity. This alignment between one's values and actions, this striving towards moral excellence, is seen as the pathway to a truly meaningful and fulfilling life.

However, the path of virtue is rarely straightforward. Life presents us with complex situations where discerning the most virtuous course of action can be challenging. What happens when virtues seem to conflict, such as when honesty clashes with compassion? Virtue ethics acknowledges these complexities, encouraging us to engage in ongoing reflection and dialogue to refine our understanding of these virtues and how they interact in different contexts.

Furthermore, the virtues themselves can be understood and prioritized differently across cultures and societies. What one culture might consider courageous, another might deem reckless. This diversity highlights the importance of engaging in cross-cultural dialogue and understanding to gain a more nuanced and comprehensive perspective on virtue.

Despite these challenges, virtue ethics offers a compelling framework for cultivating moral coherence in our lives. It calls us to look inward, to examine our values, and to strive towards becoming the best versions of ourselves. By nurturing virtues like compassion, honesty, and wisdom, we can cultivate a moral compass that guides us not just in our actions but in all aspects of our being.

Virtue ethics, then, is not about achieving moral perfection, but about embarking on a lifelong journey of self-cultivation, continually striving to refine our character and live in greater alignment with our deepest values. It's about recognizing that true moral growth comes not from following external rules but from nurturing the seeds of virtue within, allowing them to blossom into a life of meaning, purpose, and ethical excellence.

Chapter 2: Interference Patterns in Applied Ethics

Bioethics Genetic Engineering and the Diffraction of Human Nature

Imagine a world where the very essence of human nature, once thought immutable, becomes malleable in the hands of science. This is the brave new world ushered in by genetic engineering, a field teeming with both promise and peril. Like a prism diffracting a beam of light, genetic engineering refracts our understanding of human nature, splitting it into a spectrum of possibilities previously unimaginable. It grants us the power to reshape the building blocks of life, to rewrite the genetic code that defines who we are and what we might become.

On one hand, this newfound power holds immense potential for alleviating human suffering. Genetic diseases that have plagued families for generations could be eradicated, their devastating effects erased from the human experience. Imagine a world without cystic fibrosis, Huntington's disease, or sickle cell anemia — a world where children are no longer fated to inherit the genetic misfortunes of their ancestors. The potential benefits to human health and well-being are undeniable.

But this ability to manipulate our genetic blueprint also forces us to confront profound ethical questions. Where do we draw the line between therapy and enhancement? Is it ethical to use genetic engineering not just to cure diseases but to enhance desirable traits, such as intelligence, athleticism, or even physical appearance? What about the potential for exacerbating existing social inequalities, creating a world where the genetically privileged further distance themselves from the have-nots?

The ethical terrain becomes even more treacherous when we consider the potential impact on future generations. Germline editing, a technique that alters the DNA of reproductive cells, could result in genetic changes passed down to future generations, permanently altering the human gene pool. This raises the specter of unintended consequences, of unforeseen genetic vulnerabilities rippling through generations, forever altering the course of human evolution.

Furthermore, the very act of manipulating human nature in this way raises fundamental questions about our understanding of human dignity and the sanctity of life. Is there an inherent value in the diversity of human traits, even those we deem undesirable? Does the pursuit of genetic "perfection" risk devaluing those who don't conform to these manufactured ideals? And what does it mean to be "human" in a world where our genetic makeup becomes increasingly subject to human design?

These are not merely hypothetical concerns. As genetic engineering technologies rapidly advance, these ethical dilemmas are moving from the realm of science fiction to the forefront of public discourse. We are faced with a profound responsibility to carefully consider the implications of these technologies, to ensure that they are used ethically and responsibly, guided by a deep respect for human dignity and the well-being of future generations.

The diffraction of human nature through genetic engineering presents us with a kaleidoscope of possibilities, each with its own set of ethical implications. Navigating this complex landscape requires thoughtful deliberation, open dialogue, and a willingness to grapple with the profound ethical questions at the heart of this scientific revolution. It demands that we approach these technologies with both a sense of awe and a healthy dose of caution, recognizing that the choices we make today will shape the genetic legacy of humanity for generations to come.

Environmental Ethics Sustainable Development and the Interference of Needs

Picture a world where the rhythms of nature are not seen as obstacles to conquer but as the very pulse of our existence. This is the vision driving the concept of sustainable development, a delicate dance between meeting our present needs and safeguarding the needs of future generations. Yet, navigating this path toward a harmonious coexistence with our planet requires careful consideration of competing needs, a complex ethical calculus where the interests of humans and the natural world often intersect and collide.

At the heart of this ethical dilemma lies the question of responsibility. Do we, as the current stewards of

Earth, have a moral obligation to future generations to leave behind a planet capable of sustaining life in all its richness and diversity? Or are we justified in prioritizing our own immediate needs, even if it means depleting resources, disrupting ecosystems, and leaving behind a legacy of environmental degradation for future generations to inherit?

The stakes are high, and the answers are far from simple. The demands of a growing global population, coupled with rising standards of living, place an unprecedented strain on our planet's finite resources. Forests fall to make way for farmland, oceans are depleted of fish to satisfy our insatiable appetites, and the very air we breathe becomes thick with pollutants from our industries. The consequences are already being felt, from more frequent and severe weather events to mass extinctions and the displacement of communities due to rising sea levels.

Sustainable development calls for a paradigm shift, a move away from the short-sighted pursuit of immediate gratification toward a more holistic and long-term perspective. It requires recognizing the interconnectedness of all living things, acknowledging that human well-being is inextricably linked to the health of our planet. This means finding ways to meet our needs without compromising the ability of future generations to meet their own.

But how do we balance these competing needs, especially when the needs of the present often seem at odds with the needs of the future? Developing nations, struggling to lift their populations out of poverty, may prioritize economic growth over environmental protection, arguing that developed nations, having already benefited from industrialization, bear a greater responsibility for addressing climate change. Conversely, some argue that developing nations, with their rapidly growing populations and economies, will be the primary drivers of future environmental impact and therefore must be equally committed to sustainable practices.

Furthermore, the very definition of "need" becomes a point of contention. Are we talking about basic survival needs, such as food, water, and shelter, or do we include things like access to education, healthcare, and economic opportunity? And how do we weigh the needs of humans against the needs of other species and the health of ecosystems?

Navigating this ethical minefield requires a nuanced approach that acknowledges the complexities and competing interests at play. It demands open dialogue, empathy, and a willingness to compromise. It requires us to move beyond simplistic notions of right and wrong and embrace the messy reality of finding solutions that balance human needs with the long-term health of our planet.

Ultimately, the pursuit of sustainable development is not merely an environmental imperative but a moral one. It is about recognizing our interconnectedness with all living things and embracing our responsibility to be good stewards of our planet. It is about ensuring that future generations inherit a world where they too can thrive, a world where the rhythms of nature continue to sustain life in all its beauty and diversity.

Chapter 3: The Moral Spectrum: Individual and Collective Wavelengths

Cognitive Biases Distortions in our Moral Lenses

Imagine looking through a pair of glasses that subtly distort the world around you, bending light in ways you barely perceive. These are our cognitive biases, mental shortcuts hardwired into our brains through evolution, shaping our perceptions and influencing our judgments, often without our conscious awareness. While these mental shortcuts can be useful in navigating the complexities of daily life, they can also lead to systematic errors in thinking, distorting our moral lenses and leading us to make unethical decisions, all while believing we are acting rationally and morally.

One such bias is confirmation bias, our tendency to seek out and interpret information in a way that confirms our preexisting beliefs, while conveniently ignoring or downplaying evidence that contradicts our views. Imagine scrolling through your social media feed, effortlessly filtering out news and opinions that clash with your own, while readily accepting anything that aligns with your worldview. This selective exposure creates an echo chamber, reinforcing our biases and making it difficult to engage in objective moral reasoning.

Another powerful bias is the in-group/out-group bias, our tendency to favor those we perceive as part of our group, whether based on nationality, religion, political affiliation, or even something as arbitrary as our favorite sports team. This bias can lead us to judge the actions of those within our group more leniently, while holding those outside our group to a different standard. Such biased perceptions can have profound moral implications, fueling prejudice, discrimination, and even violence against those perceived as "other."

The framing effect demonstrates how the way information is presented, or framed, can dramatically influence our choices, even when the underlying options are objectively the same. Imagine being presented with two potential medical treatments, one described as having a 90% survival rate, the other as having a 10% mortality rate. While both options convey the same information, the framing significantly impacts our perception of risk and influences our decision-making. This bias highlights how subtle changes in wording or emphasis can manipulate our moral judgments, leading us to make different choices based solely on how the information is presented.

The availability heuristic, another cognitive culprit, leads us to overestimate the likelihood of events that are easily recalled, often because they are vivid, emotionally charged, or have received significant media attention. For instance, after a highly publicized plane crash, people may overestimate the dangers of air travel, even though statistically, it remains one of the safest modes of transportation. This bias can distort our moral judgments by making us overly fearful of statistically unlikely events, while neglecting more significant but less salient risks.

These are just a few examples of the many cognitive biases that can cloud our moral judgment. The anchoring bias, the halo effect, the sunk cost fallacy – each of these mental shortcuts can lead us astray, distorting our perceptions and influencing our choices in ways that deviate from our ethical ideals.

So how can we overcome these cognitive pitfalls and make more ethical decisions? Awareness is key. By understanding how these biases operate, we can begin to recognize their influence on our thinking and take steps to mitigate their impact. Seeking out diverse perspectives, challenging our own assumptions, and engaging in critical self-reflection are all crucial steps in debiasing our moral lenses.

Ultimately, ethical decision-making requires constant vigilance. It demands that we cultivate intellectual humility, acknowledging our inherent biases and remaining open to challenging our own perspectives. By recognizing the distortions in our moral lenses, we can strive to make more informed, objective, and ethical choices, aligning our actions with our values and creating a more just and compassionate world.

Cultural Relativity The Shifting Baselines of Morality

Imagine traveling to a distant land with customs and beliefs vastly different from your own. What you find shocking or taboo might be considered perfectly acceptable, even celebrated, in this new environment. This is the essence of cultural relativity, the understanding that moral values and ethical codes are not universal constants but rather fluid constructs, shaped by the unique history, traditions, and social norms of a particular culture. While this concept encourages empathy and understanding across cultures, it also presents a profound ethical challenge: how do we navigate a world where the very definition of right and wrong shifts beneath our feet?

The concept of cultural relativity encourages us to step outside the confines of our own cultural bubble and view the world through the eyes of others. It reminds us that our way of life is not the only way, nor necessarily the "right" way, simply one of many diverse expressions of human existence. This perspective is essential in fostering cross-cultural understanding and respect, counteracting ethnocentrism and promoting tolerance in an increasingly interconnected world.

However, embracing cultural relativity does not require abandoning our own moral compass or accepting all cultural practices as equally valid. There is a danger in taking cultural relativism to an extreme, falling into the trap of moral nihilism where anything goes, and no action can be judged as inherently right or wrong. This approach risks paralyzing us in the face of injustice, rendering us unable to condemn even the most egregious human rights violations if they are deemed culturally acceptable within a particular society.

The challenge, then, lies in finding a balance, a nuanced approach that acknowledges the diversity of moral frameworks while still upholding universal ethical principles that transcend cultural boundaries. This means recognizing that while certain practices may be considered morally acceptable within a particular cultural context, they may still violate fundamental human rights or cause unnecessary suffering.

For example, while some cultures may condone corporal punishment of children, scientific evidence overwhelmingly suggests that such practices are harmful to a child's physical and psychological well-being. Similarly, while certain traditions may perpetuate gender inequality or discrimination based on caste, religion, or sexual orientation, these practices clearly violate the fundamental human right to equality and dignity.

Navigating this ethical terrain requires careful consideration, open dialogue, and a willingness to engage with diverse perspectives. It demands that we approach cultural differences with both humility and critical thinking, recognizing that even deeply ingrained cultural practices can be harmful and require examination.

One approach is to focus on the underlying values and principles that inform different moral codes. While the specific expressions of these values may vary across cultures, the core principles themselves, such as fairness, compassion, and respect for human dignity, often resonate across cultural boundaries. By identifying these shared values, we can begin to build bridges of understanding and work towards common ground, even when faced with seemingly irreconcilable cultural differences.

Ultimately, embracing cultural relativity does not mean abandoning our own moral compass but rather refining it through exposure to diverse perspectives. It is about recognizing the fluidity of moral norms while holding fast to our shared humanity, striving to create a world where respect for cultural diversity goes hand in hand with the unwavering pursuit of justice and human dignity for all.

Universal Values Searching for the Constant in the Moral Equation

Is there a moral compass that points north for all humankind, a set of universal values that transcend the dizzying array of cultures, beliefs, and individual perspectives? The search for such constants in the moral equation has occupied philosophers and theologians for centuries, fueling passionate debates and shaping the very fabric of human societies. While the answer remains elusive, the very act of seeking these universal values is essential to fostering a more just, compassionate, and harmonious world.

One approach to uncovering these universal values lies in examining the common threads that weave through the diverse tapestry of human experience. Across cultures and throughout history, certain fundamental values consistently emerge as essential for peaceful coexistence and social harmony. These include:

- **Empathy and Compassion:** The ability to understand and share the feelings of others, to recognize the inherent dignity and worth of every human being, forms the bedrock of a just and compassionate society. From the Golden Rule found in various religious and ethical traditions to the modern concept of human rights, the imperative to treat others as we would wish to be treated resonates deeply across cultures.

- **Fairness and Justice:** The pursuit of fairness, the equitable distribution of resources and opportunities, and the impartial application of rules are essential for a stable and harmonious society. Whether enshrined in legal codes or upheld through social norms, the principle of justice seeks to ensure that everyone has an equal opportunity to thrive and that wrongs are addressed through fair and impartial means.

- **Truthfulness and Honesty:** Trust forms the foundation of any healthy relationship, be it between individuals, communities, or nations. Truthfulness, honesty, and integrity are essential for building and maintaining that trust, fostering open communication, and creating an environment where cooperation and mutual respect can flourish.

- **Responsibility and Accountability:** Recognizing our interconnectedness and taking responsibility for our actions are crucial for a sustainable and just world. This includes accountability not only for our individual choices but also for the collective impact of our actions on others, future generations, and the planet we share.

While these values may find expression in different ways across cultures, their underlying principles remain remarkably consistent. They reflect a shared understanding of what it means to be human, to live in community with others, and to navigate the complexities of the human experience with empathy, integrity, and a commitment to justice.

However, the search for universal values is not without its challenges. Cultural differences, historical contexts, and individual interpretations can all influence how these values are understood and applied. Moreover, the very act of defining and prioritizing certain values inevitably involves subjective judgments and potential biases.

Despite these challenges, the pursuit of universal values remains a worthwhile endeavor. By engaging in open and respectful dialogue, by listening to diverse perspectives and seeking common ground, we can move closer to a shared understanding of our common humanity and the ethical principles that can guide us towards a more just and compassionate world.

The search for universal values is not about imposing a rigid or monolithic moral code but rather about fostering a shared ethical framework that can guide our interactions, inform our decision-making, and inspire us to create a world where everyone has the opportunity to thrive. It is a journey of continuous learning, reflection, and dialogue, a journey that requires us to embrace our shared humanity while respecting the rich tapestry of cultures and beliefs that make us unique.

Chapter 4: The Ethics of Artificial Intelligence Measuring the Morality of Machines

Algorithmic Bias Reflecting and Amplifying Human Prejudice

Algorithms, those intricate lines of code that increasingly govern our digital lives, hold the promise of objectivity and efficiency. They sift through mountains of data, identify patterns, and make decisions at a scale and speed unattainable by humans. Yet, beneath this veneer of impartiality lies a disconcerting truth: algorithms can inherit and even amplify the biases present in the data they are trained on, perpetuating and exacerbating existing social inequalities.

Imagine an algorithm designed to assist companies in their hiring process. It sifts through resumes, analyzes qualifications, and recommends the most promising candidates. Seems fair, right? However, if this algorithm is trained on data from a company with a history of discriminatory hiring practices, it may learn to associate success with certain demographic characteristics, inadvertently perpetuating those biases in future hiring decisions. The algorithm, blind to the social context and historical injustices embedded in the data, becomes an unwitting accomplice in perpetuating discrimination.

This phenomenon, known as algorithmic bias, arises from the fact that algorithms are only as good as the data they are fed. If the training data reflects existing societal biases, whether conscious or unconscious, the algorithm will inherit and potentially amplify those biases in its outputs. This can have far-reaching consequences, impacting everything from loan approvals and insurance rates to criminal justice outcomes and access to healthcare.

Consider the case of facial recognition technology. Studies have shown that some facial recognition algorithms exhibit significantly higher error rates for individuals with darker skin tones, particularly women. This disparity arises from the fact that these algorithms are often trained on datasets that are not representative of the diversity of human faces, leading to biased outcomes that can have serious implications, particularly in law enforcement contexts where misidentification can have life-altering consequences.

The issue extends beyond biased datasets. The very design of an algorithm, the choices made by its creators in terms of what data to use, how to define success, and what factors to prioritize, can all introduce or exacerbate bias. For instance, an algorithm designed to predict recidivism rates, used by some judges in sentencing decisions, might inadvertently perpetuate racial biases if it relies heavily on factors like zip codes or prior arrest records, which can be correlated with race due to systemic inequalities in law enforcement practices.

Addressing algorithmic bias requires a multi-pronged approach. First and foremost, it demands greater transparency and accountability in the development and deployment of algorithms. This includes auditing algorithms for bias, making the code and training data publicly available for scrutiny, and establishing clear lines of responsibility for addressing instances of bias.

Secondly, we need to diversify the teams designing and developing these algorithms. A more inclusive tech industry, with representation from diverse backgrounds and perspectives, is crucial for identifying and mitigating potential biases that might otherwise go unnoticed.

Finally, we must address the root causes of societal biases that find their way into our data. This requires a broader societal effort to combat discrimination, promote equality, and create a more just and equitable world, both online and offline.

Algorithmic bias is not an insurmountable problem, but it is a complex one that requires our attention and action. By acknowledging the potential for bias, by demanding transparency and accountability, and by working to create a more just and equitable society, we can harness the power of algorithms for good, ensuring that these technologies serve to empower all members of society, rather than perpetuate existing inequalities.

Machine Learning and Moral Agency Can AI Develop its Own Wavelength

As machines grow increasingly sophisticated, mimicking and even surpassing human capabilities in complex tasks, a fundamental question arises: can they develop their own moral agency, their own sense of right and wrong? Can a machine, even one capable of learning and adapting, ever truly understand the nuances of human values and make ethical decisions on its own terms?

The question of machine morality is inextricably linked to the concept of agency. When we speak of moral agency, we refer to the capacity for making deliberate choices based on an understanding of ethical principles and their consequences. It implies an awareness of oneself as an entity capable of affecting the world, coupled with a sense of responsibility for those actions.

While machines can be programmed to follow pre-defined rules and optimize for specific outcomes, this does not necessarily equate to moral agency. A machine tasked with maximizing efficiency in a factory setting, for instance, might prioritize output over worker safety if those parameters are not explicitly defined in its programming. It operates based on a set of instructions, not on an intrinsic understanding of the ethical implications of its actions.

However, the advent of machine learning introduces a new dimension to this debate. Unlike traditional algorithms that follow pre-programmed instructions, machine learning systems learn from data, identifying patterns and adapting their behavior accordingly. This ability to learn and evolve independently raises the intriguing possibility of machines developing their own internal frameworks for decision-making, frameworks that might encompass ethical considerations.

Imagine a machine learning system designed to assist doctors in diagnosing and treating patients. As it processes vast amounts of medical data, it might begin to identify patterns and correlations that go beyond its initial programming. It might learn to prioritize patient well-being over mere adherence to medical protocols, making nuanced judgments based on its growing understanding of human health and suffering.

While this example suggests the potential for machines to develop a form of ethical reasoning, it also highlights the challenges inherent in this endeavor. Human morality is not simply a matter of logic and pattern recognition; it is deeply intertwined with our emotions, our social interactions, and our shared cultural and historical experiences. Can a machine, even one capable of sophisticated learning, ever truly grasp the complexities of human values and the subjective nature of ethical dilemmas?

Moreover, the question of machine morality raises profound ethical questions about responsibility and accountability. If a machine makes a decision that results in harm, who is ultimately responsible? The programmers who designed the algorithm? The users who deployed it? Or could the machine itself be held accountable for its actions?

As we navigate the uncharted waters of increasingly sophisticated machines, the question of machine morality will continue to challenge our assumptions about consciousness, agency, and the very nature of ethical decision-making. While definitive answers remain elusive, grappling with these questions is essential for ensuring that the development and deployment of these technologies align with our values and contribute to a more just and equitable future.

The path forward lies in fostering interdisciplinary dialogue, involving ethicists, philosophers, and social scientists alongside computer scientists and engineers. By carefully considering the ethical implications of our creations, by embedding human values into their design, and by remaining vigilant about the potential for unintended consequences, we can strive to ensure that as machines become more intelligent, they also become more ethical, contributing to a future where technology serves humanity in all its complexity.

The Future of Ethical AI Designing for Transparency and Accountability

As we stand on the cusp of an era defined by increasingly sophisticated machines, the need to ensure those machines operate ethically becomes paramount. The challenge lies not just in preventing harm, but in proactively designing systems that embody our values, systems that are transparent, accountable, and aligned with the best of human aspirations. The future of ethical technology hinges on our ability to build these principles into the very fabric of their design.

Transparency, in the context of complex systems, can feel like a slippery concept. It's not simply about making code publicly available, though that can be a part of it. True transparency involves clarity around purpose. Why was a particular system created? What need does it aim to address, and how were those needs determined? This requires open dialogue between creators, users, and those potentially impacted by a technology, ensuring diverse voices contribute to its definition of success.

Moreover, transparency demands explainability. Can we understand the decision-making processes of these systems, particularly when those decisions have significant consequences? This is especially crucial for systems utilizing complex learning algorithms, where the reasoning behind specific outputs may be opaque even to their creators. Developing methods for auditing these systems, for generating clear and understandable explanations for their actions, is essential for building trust and ensuring accountability.

Accountability, in essence, means ensuring that when things go wrong — as they inevitably will in any complex system — there are mechanisms for identifying responsibility and seeking redress. This requires moving beyond the simplistic notion of machines as blameless actors. We must ask: who benefits from the system's successes, and who bears the burden when it fails? Are there clear lines of responsibility, both for preventing harm and for addressing it when it occurs?

Establishing accountability might involve rethinking our legal frameworks and regulatory structures. Traditional models of liability may prove inadequate for addressing the unique challenges posed by complex, learning systems. We need to explore new approaches, potentially involving shared responsibility among creators, deployers, and even users, with clear mechanisms for addressing harms and providing recourse.

However, designing for ethical AI goes beyond mere compliance with rules or avoidance of harm. It's about actively embedding positive values into these systems. If we want technology that promotes fairness, we need to design systems that explicitly account for historical biases and strive for equitable outcomes. If we value human autonomy, we need to design systems that empower individuals, providing meaningful control over their data and how it is used.

This requires a shift in perspective, from viewing ethics as a constraint on innovation to recognizing it as a catalyst for more thoughtful, human-centered design. It requires investing in interdisciplinary collaboration, bringing together ethicists, social scientists, and legal experts alongside technologists and engineers. It demands we prioritize long-term societal impact alongside immediate technical achievements.

The path forward is not one of relinquishing control to machines, but of shaping their development with intention and foresight. It's about recognizing that the true potential of these technologies lies not just in their ability to perform tasks, but in their capacity to augment our own moral imaginations, to help us build a future that reflects our highest aspirations for ourselves and for humanity as a whole.

Chapter 5: The Moral Landscape: Navigating Complex Ethical Dilemmas

The Trolley Problem Revisited Analyzing Interference Patterns in Decision Making

The trolley problem, a thought experiment that has haunted ethics discussions for decades, presents a stark moral dilemma: would you sacrifice one life to save five? The classic scenario involves a runaway trolley barreling towards five unsuspecting individuals. You, a bystander, have the power to divert the trolley onto a side track, where it would kill one person instead. Do you intervene, choosing one death over five, or do you abstain, allowing the tragedy to unfold?

While seemingly abstract, the trolley problem highlights the complexities of ethical decision-making, particularly when forced to choose between two undesirable outcomes. It compels us to confront our values, weighing utilitarian calculations of maximizing overall well-being against moral principles like the inherent value of each human life.

But what happens when we introduce the intricate workings of complex systems into this ethical quagmire? As we increasingly rely on algorithms to make decisions, understanding how these systems navigate such dilemmas becomes crucial. Instead of a singular, conscious choice, we encounter a web of calculations, data points, and pre-programmed objectives, creating interference patterns that ripple through the decision-making process.

Imagine a self-driving car facing a real-world trolley problem. An unavoidable collision is imminent, with multiple potential trajectories, each resulting in different outcomes for passengers and pedestrians. How does the car's navigation system, trained on vast datasets of traffic patterns and accident scenarios, determine the "least harmful" course of action?

Unlike the human bystander grappling with moral principles, the algorithm operates within the confines of its programming. It analyzes data points: proximity of pedestrians, speed of the vehicle, potential for injury based on crash simulations. It identifies patterns, calculating probabilities of minimizing harm based on its training data. But can it truly grasp the weight of human life, the emotional toll of loss, the ethical nuances that permeate such a situation?

This is where the interference patterns become apparent. The algorithm's decision, seemingly objective and data-driven, is shaped by a multitude of factors: the biases inherent in its training data, the priorities set by its programmers, the design choices made in its risk assessment models. These factors, often invisible to the end-user, create ripples that distort the ethical landscape, leading to outcomes that may not align with our intuitive understanding of right and wrong.

Furthermore, the speed at which these decisions are made adds another layer of complexity. Human deliberation, fraught with emotional turmoil and moral wrestling, is replaced by instantaneous calculations. The algorithm, devoid of emotional burden, acts swiftly, guided by its programmed objectives, but potentially overlooking the nuanced ethical considerations that would factor into a human's decision.

Analyzing these interference patterns requires a shift in perspective. We can no longer rely solely on traditional ethical frameworks designed for human agency. We must develop new tools and methodologies for understanding the decision-making processes of complex systems, for identifying potential biases, and for ensuring that these systems operate within acceptable ethical boundaries.

This involves fostering greater transparency in algorithm design, allowing for scrutiny of training data and decision-making logic. It necessitates developing methods for explaining algorithmic outcomes in clear, understandable terms, bridging the gap between complex computations and human comprehension. And it demands ongoing ethical reflection, a continuous dialogue between technologists, ethicists, and the public to ensure that these systems align with our values as we navigate an increasingly automated world.

The trolley problem, once a thought experiment confined to philosophy classrooms, is now a tangible challenge in the age of intelligent machines. By understanding the interference patterns inherent in algorithmic decision-making, by demanding transparency and accountability, and by fostering ongoing ethical reflection, we can strive to create systems that navigate these dilemmas responsibly, maximizing benefit while minimizing harm, and ultimately, building a future where technology serves humanity in all its complexity.

War and Peace The Ethics of Force and the Diffraction of Justice

War, a brutal dance of destruction and despair, has been a grim companion to humanity throughout history. Peace, its elusive counterpart, represents a yearning for harmony and stability, a world where swords are beaten into plowshares and dialogue replaces the din of battle. Yet, as we navigate an era of unprecedented technological advancement, the lines between war and peace blur, and the very concept of justice, once seemingly clear-cut, undergoes a profound diffraction.

The ethics of force, traditionally rooted in principles of just war theory, grapple with the justification for resorting to violence, the permissible means of conducting warfare, and the moral obligations towards both combatants and non-combatants. Yet, these principles, forged in the crucible of historical conflicts, are strained when confronted with the realities of modern warfare.

Drones, guided by algorithms and piloted remotely, can strike with pinpoint accuracy, minimizing collateral damage. Cyberwarfare, waged in the ethereal realm of digital networks, can cripple infrastructure and sow chaos without firing a single shot. Autonomous weapons systems, poised to revolutionize the battlefield, promise to remove human emotion from the equation, potentially reducing impulsive acts of cruelty.

But these technological advancements, while seemingly offering a path towards more "humane" warfare, also raise profound ethical dilemmas. The distance afforded by remote warfare can create a disconnect between action and consequence, potentially lowering the threshold for resorting to force. Cyberattacks, while often bloodless, can have devastating real-world impacts, disrupting critical services and undermining societal trust. And the prospect of autonomous weapons, capable of making life-or-death decisions without human intervention, challenges our very understanding of moral responsibility on the battlefield.

Furthermore, the traditional boundaries between war and peace have become increasingly porous. Cyber intrusions, disinformation campaigns, and economic warfare blur the lines between overt conflict and simmering tensions. The constant threat of violence, even if not actively realized, casts a long shadow, eroding trust, fueling instability, and hindering the pursuit of lasting peace.

In this complex and interconnected world, the diffraction of justice becomes glaringly apparent. Who is held accountable for the unintended consequences of cyberattacks, for the collateral damage inflicted by drone strikes, for the decisions made by autonomous weapons? How do we ensure proportionality and discrimination in conflicts waged across multiple domains, where the lines between combatant and civilian are often blurred?

Traditional legal frameworks, designed for a world of clearly defined nation-states and conventional warfare, struggle to keep pace with these evolving realities. International cooperation, already fraught with challenges, becomes even more crucial in establishing norms and regulations for emerging technologies, ensuring their development and deployment adhere to ethical principles.

Moreover, the pursuit of peace demands a more nuanced and holistic approach. It requires addressing the root causes of conflict, from poverty and inequality to political oppression and historical grievances. It necessitates investing in diplomacy, conflict resolution mechanisms, and cross-cultural understanding, fostering dialogue and building bridges of trust across divides.

The ethics of force in the 21st century cannot be divorced from the pursuit of justice and the imperative for peace. As technology reshapes the landscape of conflict, we must ensure that our values, our principles, and our commitment to a more just and peaceful world guide our every step. The path forward lies not in seeking technological solutions to inherently human problems, but in leveraging our ingenuity, compassion, and collective wisdom to create a future where war becomes a relic of the past and peace, however elusive, remains our unwavering goal.

Global Poverty and Inequality Reconciling Competing Moral Obligations

The stark reality of global poverty casts a long shadow over our collective conscience. Millions endure the daily struggle for survival, lacking access to basic necessities like food, clean water, healthcare, and education. This immense suffering coexists with unprecedented wealth and technological advancement, a stark testament to the deeply ingrained inequalities that permeate our world. Reconciling our moral obligations to alleviate this suffering, while navigating the complexities of global interconnectedness, demands a nuanced and multifaceted approach.

At the heart of this challenge lies a fundamental ethical dilemma: do we prioritize the immediate needs of those suffering in poverty, or do we focus on addressing the systemic issues that perpetuate inequality? Both perspectives carry significant moral weight, leading to competing obligations that defy easy solutions.

On one hand, the urgency of poverty compels immediate action. Providing food, shelter, and medical care can make a tangible difference in the lives of those struggling to survive. Humanitarian aid, disaster relief efforts, and development programs targeting specific needs all play a crucial role in alleviating suffering and empowering communities.

However, simply addressing the symptoms of poverty without tackling its root causes risks perpetuating a cycle of dependence. Systemic issues like unfair trade practices, exploitative labor conditions, and unequal access to resources create barriers that prevent individuals and communities from lifting themselves out of poverty. Addressing these systemic issues requires a long-term perspective, focusing on sustainable solutions that empower individuals and foster self-reliance.

This is where the concept of global interconnectedness comes into play. The decisions made in one corner of the world can have ripple effects, impacting the lives of people thousands of miles away. Trade agreements, for example, can either reinforce existing power imbalances or create opportunities for developing countries to participate in the global economy on a more equitable footing. Similarly, environmental policies can either exacerbate climate change, disproportionately impacting vulnerable communities, or promote sustainable practices that benefit all.

Reconciling our competing moral obligations requires recognizing this interconnectedness and embracing a sense of shared responsibility. Developed nations, often historically complicit in creating and perpetuating global inequality, bear a particular obligation to assist developing countries in their efforts to achieve economic and social progress. This assistance should go beyond traditional aid, encompassing fair trade practices, debt relief, and technology transfer that empowers local communities.

Moreover, it is crucial to recognize that solutions to poverty and inequality cannot be imposed from above.

Local communities must be active participants in the development process, their voices heard, their needs understood, and their knowledge respected. Empowering women, who often bear the brunt of poverty, is essential, as investing in their education and economic opportunities has a multiplier effect, benefiting families and communities as a whole.

Technology, while not a panacea, can play a transformative role in this endeavor. From mobile banking platforms that provide financial inclusion to telemedicine initiatives that extend healthcare access to remote areas, technology can bridge gaps and empower communities. However, it is essential to ensure that technological advancements are deployed ethically and equitably, avoiding the creation of new digital divides that exacerbate existing inequalities.

Ultimately, reconciling our competing moral obligations requires a fundamental shift in perspective. It demands moving beyond a charity-based approach to one rooted in solidarity and shared humanity. It necessitates recognizing that our own well-being is inextricably linked to the well-being of others, regardless of geographical boundaries. By embracing this interconnectedness, by working collaboratively to address both the symptoms and root causes of poverty and inequality, we can create a more just and equitable world for all.

Chapter 6: The Evolution of Ethics: From Biological Imperatives to Moral Progress

The Origins of Morality Evolutionary Roots and Social Instincts

Morality, with its intricate tapestry of rules, values, and beliefs about right and wrong, has long been a subject of intense philosophical and theological debate. Yet, beneath the layers of cultural norms and religious doctrines lies a fascinating biological foundation, a testament to the evolutionary roots and social instincts that have shaped our moral sense. Understanding these origins provides valuable insights into the nature of morality itself, revealing its universality, its adaptability, and its profound connection to our evolutionary heritage.

From a purely biological perspective, morality might seem like an anomaly. Natural selection, the driving force of evolution, favors traits that enhance an organism's chances of survival and reproduction. How, then, could altruism, empathy, and a sense of fairness—traits that often require self-sacrifice and benefit others—have evolved?

The answer lies in the complex interplay between genes and behavior, individual fitness and group survival. While selfish behavior might benefit an individual in the short term, a group composed solely of self-serving individuals is inherently unstable.

Cooperation, on the other hand, allows groups to share resources, protect themselves from threats, and raise offspring more effectively. Thus, over time, groups with a higher proportion of cooperative individuals would have outcompeted their more selfish counterparts, leading to the gradual spread of prosocial traits.

Evidence for this evolutionary basis of morality can be found in the behavior of other social animals, particularly our primate cousins. Chimpanzees, for example, engage in reciprocal altruism, grooming each other and sharing food with those who have helped them in the past. They also exhibit a rudimentary sense of fairness, protesting when they receive a less desirable reward than a peer for performing the same task.

In humans, these social instincts have been refined and elaborated through the process of cultural evolution. As our ancestors formed larger and more complex societies, the need for rules and norms to regulate behavior became increasingly important. Moral codes, often intertwined with religious beliefs, provided a framework for cooperation, conflict resolution, and social cohesion.

Language played a crucial role in this process, allowing us to communicate our values, share our experiences, and transmit moral teachings across generations. Stories, myths, and religious parables served as powerful tools for instilling moral values, providing concrete examples of right and wrong behavior and reinforcing social norms.

Furthermore, the human capacity for empathy and perspective-taking, while rooted in our evolutionary past, has reached unparalleled heights in our species. We can imagine ourselves in the shoes of others, understand their emotions, and feel compassion for their suffering. This ability to transcend our own egocentric perspective lies at the heart of many moral principles, motivating us to treat others with kindness, fairness, and respect.

However, the evolutionary roots of morality do not imply that our moral sense is fixed or immutable. Just as our physical traits have evolved over time, so too has our moral compass. Slavery, once widely accepted, is now universally condemned. Gender equality, once a radical notion, is increasingly recognized as a fundamental human right. These shifts in moral attitudes demonstrate the adaptability of our moral sense, its capacity to evolve in response to changing social norms, cultural influences, and reasoned arguments.

Understanding the evolutionary roots of morality does not provide easy answers to complex ethical dilemmas. However, it offers a valuable framework for understanding the universality of many moral principles, their connection to our biological heritage, and their potential for both progress and regression. By acknowledging the deep-seated instincts that underpin our moral sense, we can engage in more nuanced and informed discussions about the values we hold dear, the societies we strive to create, and the future of morality itself.

Moral Progress Expanding the Circle of Concern

The annals of history paint a tumultuous picture, a tapestry woven with threads of both profound cruelty and remarkable compassion. While humans are capable of immense brutality, we also possess an innate capacity for empathy, a flickering flame that has, over millennia, illuminated a path towards a more just and humane world. This moral progress, while often halting and uneven, speaks to our ability to expand our circle of concern, extending our moral consideration beyond narrow tribal boundaries to encompass ever-wider groups.

Early human societies were characterized by a strong in-group bias. Morality was largely confined to one's own tribe or clan, with outsiders viewed with suspicion, if not outright hostility. This tribalism, while providing a sense of belonging and security within the group, often led to intergroup conflict and violence.

However, as societies grew larger and more complex, so too did our moral horizons. Trade, diplomacy, and cultural exchange fostered interaction and interdependence between different groups, gradually chipping away at the barriers of prejudice and suspicion. Empires, while often built on conquest and exploitation, also facilitated the spread of ideas and values, exposing people to different cultures and worldviews.

Religion, too, played a pivotal role in expanding the circle of concern. Many faiths preached a universal love and compassion, transcending the boundaries of tribe, nation, or ethnicity. The Golden Rule, articulated in various forms across different cultures and religions, encapsulated this ethical ideal, urging individuals to treat others as they themselves would like to be treated.

The Enlightenment, a period of unprecedented intellectual and scientific ferment, marked a turning point in the history of moral progress. Thinkers like John Locke and Immanuel Kant emphasized the inherent dignity and rights of all human beings, regardless of their social status, ethnicity, or religious beliefs. This emphasis on universal human rights laid the groundwork for the abolition of slavery, the expansion of suffrage, and the recognition of the inherent equality of all people.

The 20th century witnessed both the horrors of genocide and the rise of a global human rights movement. The atrocities of World War II, in particular, served as a stark reminder of the dangers of unchecked hatred and prejudice. In the aftermath of this global conflict, the international community came together to establish the United Nations, founded on the principles of peace, security, and respect for human rights.

The Universal Declaration of Human Rights, adopted in 1948, stands as a testament to this commitment, articulating a shared set of values and aspirations for all humankind. While the realization of these rights remains an ongoing struggle, the very existence of such a document reflects a profound shift in our collective moral consciousness.

Today, the circle of concern continues to expand, encompassing not only all humans but also the natural world. The growing awareness of our interconnectedness with the environment, coupled with the urgent threat of climate change, has spurred a global movement for environmental protection and sustainability. Animal rights, once a fringe issue, have gained increasing prominence, as more people recognize the sentience and moral worth of other species.

This expansion of our moral circle has not been without its challenges and setbacks. Tribalism, prejudice, and discrimination persist, often fueled by economic anxieties, political opportunism, and the human proclivity for fear and division. Yet, despite these challenges, the overall trajectory of human history points towards a gradual widening of our moral horizons.

From the abolition of slavery to the fight for gender equality, from the recognition of LGBTQ+ rights to the growing movement for animal welfare, we see countless examples of individuals and societies challenging the status quo, expanding their circle of concern, and striving to create a more just and compassionate world. This ongoing journey towards a more inclusive and empathetic society is a testament to the transformative power of moral progress, a testament to our capacity to learn, to grow, and to build a better future for all.

The Future of Morality Emerging Ethical Challenges in a Changing World

The 21st century unfolds before us as a period of unprecedented change, a maelstrom of technological advancements, globalization, and environmental shifts reshaping the very foundations of our societies and challenging our deeply held moral beliefs. As we navigate this complex and rapidly evolving landscape, we encounter a myriad of emerging ethical dilemmas that demand careful consideration and a willingness to adapt our moral compass to uncharted territory.

At the forefront of this ethical revolution stands the dizzying pace of technological innovation. Biotechnology, in particular, presents us with a Pandora's Box of possibilities and perils. Gene editing, for example, holds the potential to cure debilitating diseases, but it also raises profound questions about human enhancement, genetic engineering, and the very definition of what it means to be human. The development of artificial wombs could revolutionize reproductive rights, but it also compels us to grapple with the ethical implications of creating life outside the traditional bounds of biology.

Artificial intelligence, with its ever-increasing capabilities, poses equally profound ethical challenges. As algorithms become more sophisticated, they are entrusted with making decisions that have real-world consequences, from medical diagnoses to loan applications to criminal justice. Ensuring that these algorithms are designed and deployed ethically, free from bias and discrimination, is paramount to preventing the perpetuation and amplification of existing social inequalities.

The rise of autonomous weapons systems, powered by artificial intelligence, presents a particularly chilling ethical dilemma. Delegating life-or-death decisions to machines, without human oversight or intervention, challenges our fundamental understanding of morality, accountability, and the just conduct of war. International cooperation and regulation are essential to prevent an AI arms race that could have catastrophic consequences for humanity.

Globalization, while fostering interconnectedness and economic growth, also presents its own set of ethical challenges. Multinational corporations, wielding immense power and influence, operate across borders, often exploiting lax labor laws and environmental regulations in developing countries. Holding these corporations accountable for their actions, ensuring fair wages, safe working conditions, and sustainable practices, requires a global effort to establish ethical standards and enforce compliance.

Climate change, the defining crisis of our time, poses an existential threat to humanity and the natural world. Addressing this challenge demands a fundamental shift in our values and priorities, moving away from short-term economic gain towards a more sustainable and equitable model of development. The ethical imperative to act, to mitigate the worst effects of climate change, falls upon all of us, but particularly on those in positions of power and influence.

Moreover, the increasing interconnectedness of our world means that ethical dilemmas rarely respect national boundaries. Issues like global poverty, pandemics, and cybersecurity require international cooperation and a shared sense of responsibility. Developing ethical frameworks that can guide decision-making in a globalized world, balancing national interests with the common good, is an ongoing challenge.

The future of morality, in this era of unprecedented change, hinges on our ability to cultivate a sense of ethical imagination, a willingness to grapple with complex issues, to challenge our assumptions, and to adapt our moral compass to the ever-evolving landscape of the 21st century. It requires fostering dialogue and collaboration across disciplines, cultures, and generations, recognizing that the ethical challenges we face are interconnected and demand collective action.

Ultimately, the future of morality is not predetermined. It is a story that we are writing together, through our choices, our actions, and our commitment to creating a more just, equitable, and sustainable world for all.

Chapter 7: Building a More Ethical Future: Harnessing the Power of Moral Wavelengths

Moral Education Cultivating Ethical Sensitivity and Judgment

Moral education, a cornerstone of human civilization since antiquity, is not merely the transmission of rules and precepts. It is the artful cultivation of ethical sensitivity, the nurturing of our innate capacity for empathy, compassion, and reason, ultimately guiding us to make sound moral judgments. In a world awash in complexity and often grappling with shifting ethical sands, fostering this moral growth is more vital than ever.

The seeds of moral education are often sown in the fertile ground of childhood. From a tender age, we observe and absorb the values modeled by our parents, caregivers, and communities. Storytelling, a powerful tool employed for millennia, imparts moral lessons through captivating narratives, embedding ethical principles in our consciousness long before we can articulate them. The heroes we admire, the villains we abhor, and the consequences they reap, all shape our understanding of right and wrong, courage and cowardice, kindness and cruelty.

Formal education plays a crucial role in nourishing these nascent moral seedlings. Exposure to diverse perspectives, historical events, and philosophical thought broadens our understanding of the human condition, fostering empathy and challenging our preconceived notions. Literature, in particular, offers a unique window into the complexities of human motivation, the nuances of ethical dilemmas, and the profound consequences of our choices.

However, moral education extends far beyond the classroom walls and the written word. Engaging in meaningful dialogue, respectfully listening to opposing viewpoints, and thoughtfully articulating our own values are all essential practices in honing our ethical reasoning skills. Civil discourse, even when it involves disagreement, sharpens our ability to critically examine our own biases, to recognize the humanity in those with whom we differ, and to seek common ground.

Experiential learning, too, plays a vital role in moral development. Volunteering in our communities, witnessing firsthand the struggles and triumphs of others, and actively working to alleviate suffering fosters empathy and compassion. These experiences bridge the gap between theoretical knowledge and lived reality, transforming moral principles from abstract concepts into guiding forces in our lives.

Developing ethical judgment, however, requires more than just empathy and good intentions. It demands cultivating critical thinking skills, the ability to analyze complex situations, identify ethical dilemmas, and evaluate potential courses of action. This process often involves wrestling with ambiguity, recognizing that there may not always be easy answers or clear-cut solutions.

Moral dilemmas, by their very nature, present us with conflicting values, forcing us to prioritize and make difficult choices. Learning to navigate these ethical gray areas requires developing a framework for ethical decision-making, one that considers the potential consequences of our actions, the rights and interests of all stakeholders, and the long-term impact on ourselves and society.

In today's rapidly changing world, moral education must also equip us to grapple with emerging ethical challenges. Advances in technology, globalization, and environmental concerns present us with novel dilemmas that require careful consideration and a willingness to adapt our moral compass to uncharted territory. Fostering ethical sensitivity and judgment in the face of these challenges is paramount to ensuring a just and sustainable future.

Ultimately, moral education is a lifelong pursuit, a continuous process of reflection, growth, and refinement. It is about cultivating within ourselves and future generations the capacity for empathy, compassion, critical thinking, and ethical decision-making. By nurturing these qualities, we empower ourselves to navigate the complexities of the human experience, to build more just and compassionate societies, and to leave the world a better place than we found it.

Building Ethical Institutions Aligning Systems with Moral Principles

Societies, like grand tapestries, are woven from intricate threads of individual lives, relationships, and shared values. Yet, underpinning this intricate human fabric lies a framework of institutions—governments, corporations, legal systems, and social norms—that shape our collective destiny. Building ethical institutions, aligning these systems with moral principles, is paramount to creating a just, equitable, and flourishing society.

The foundation of any ethical institution rests upon the bedrock of justice. A just society ensures that all its members have equal access to basic rights and liberties, regardless of their background, beliefs, or social standing. It upholds the rule of law impartially, holding individuals and institutions accountable for their actions, and providing avenues for redress when wrongs are committed. Transparency, a cornerstone of just institutions, fosters public trust by ensuring that decisions are made openly and accountably, minimizing the potential for corruption and abuse of power.

However, justice alone is insufficient. Ethical institutions must also be compassionate, recognizing the inherent dignity and worth of every human being. Social safety nets, providing for the basic needs of the most vulnerable members of society, are not merely acts of charity but reflections of a compassionate society that values the well-being of all its citizens. Access to quality education, healthcare, and economic opportunity empowers individuals to live fulfilling lives, breaking cycles of poverty and inequality.

Ethical institutions must also be designed to promote fairness, ensuring that everyone has an equal opportunity to succeed, regardless of their starting point in life. This requires actively dismantling systemic barriers that perpetuate discrimination and disadvantage, whether based on race, gender, religion, sexual orientation, or socioeconomic status. Affirmative action policies, while often controversial, can play a vital role in leveling the playing field, providing historically marginalized groups with opportunities they might otherwise be denied.

Moreover, ethical institutions must be responsive to the needs and aspirations of the people they serve. This requires fostering participatory governance, creating mechanisms for citizens to engage in meaningful dialogue, voice their concerns, and hold their leaders accountable. Freedom of speech and assembly, cornerstones of a vibrant democracy, allow for the free exchange of ideas, dissent, and debate, essential ingredients for a healthy and evolving society.

Corporations, too, play a pivotal role in shaping the moral landscape of society. As engines of economic growth and innovation, businesses wield immense power and influence, shaping not only our material lives but also our values and aspirations. Building ethical corporations requires fostering a culture of responsibility, where profits are not pursued at the expense of ethical considerations.

Corporate social responsibility, once considered an optional add-on, is increasingly recognized as an integral part of good business practice. Consumers, investors, and employees are demanding that corporations align their operations with ethical values, from environmental sustainability to fair labor practices to responsible supply chains. This shift reflects a growing awareness that ethical behavior is not only morally right but also makes good business sense, fostering trust, enhancing brand reputation, and attracting top talent.

Building ethical institutions is not a one-time endeavor but an ongoing process, requiring constant vigilance, adaptation, and renewal. It demands a commitment to ethical leadership at all levels of society, from government officials to corporate executives to community organizers. Ethical leaders lead by example, demonstrating integrity, compassion, and a commitment to the common good. They foster a culture of ethics within their organizations, establishing clear ethical guidelines, providing ethics training, and creating mechanisms for reporting and addressing ethical concerns.

Ultimately, building ethical institutions is a collective endeavor, requiring the active participation of all members of society. It demands that we hold ourselves and each other accountable for upholding ethical principles, challenging injustice, and advocating for a more just, equitable, and compassionate world. The task may be daunting, but the stakes could not be higher. For it is in the crucible of ethical institutions that we forge the kind of society we aspire to be, one that reflects our highest values and aspirations.

The Role of Technology Amplifying Ethical Action and Promoting Moral Progress

Technology, a double-edged sword forged in the fires of human ingenuity, has the capacity to both elevate and erode our moral landscape. While often viewed through a lens of progress and innovation, its ethical implications demand careful consideration. Used wisely, technology can serve as a powerful tool for amplifying ethical action, promoting moral progress, and building a more just and compassionate world.

One of the most profound ways technology amplifies ethical action is by fostering transparency and accountability. The ubiquitous nature of smartphones, equipped with cameras and internet access, has empowered ordinary citizens to document and expose injustice, corruption, and human rights abuses, holding individuals and institutions accountable in ways unimaginable just a generation ago. Social media platforms, while not without their flaws, have provided a global megaphone for marginalized voices to be heard, sparking movements for social change and challenging entrenched power structures.

Moreover, technology can facilitate ethical decision-making by providing access to information and diverse perspectives. Online educational resources, open-access journals, and virtual libraries have democratized knowledge, empowering individuals to educate themselves on complex ethical issues and engage in informed debate. Crowdsourcing platforms can tap into the collective wisdom of diverse communities, generating innovative solutions to ethical challenges and fostering a sense of shared responsibility.

Technology can also amplify ethical action by connecting individuals and organizations working towards common goals. Social networking platforms have proven to be powerful tools for organizing volunteers, mobilizing resources, and coordinating efforts across geographical boundaries. Non-profit organizations, armed with sophisticated digital tools, can reach wider audiences, raise funds more effectively, and measure their impact with greater precision.

Furthermore, technology can promote moral progress by fostering empathy and understanding across cultures. Virtual reality experiences, for example, can transport individuals to distant lands, immersing them in the lives and struggles of others. Such immersive experiences can break down prejudices, foster compassion, and inspire action by bridging the gap between "us" and "them."

Technology can also play a vital role in promoting environmental sustainability, a pressing moral imperative of our time. Precision agriculture, powered by sensors, data analytics, and artificial intelligence, can optimize crop yields while minimizing water and pesticide use. Renewable energy technologies, from solar panels to wind turbines, offer sustainable alternatives to fossil fuels, mitigating the impacts of climate change.

However, the ethical implications of technology are not always straightforward. The same tools that can amplify ethical action can also be used for nefarious purposes. Social media platforms, while connecting individuals across borders, can also be used to spread misinformation, incite hatred, and manipulate public opinion. Data privacy concerns, algorithmic bias, and the potential for job displacement due to automation are just a few of the ethical challenges posed by emerging technologies.

Therefore, harnessing the power of technology for moral progress requires a thoughtful and proactive approach. We must develop ethical frameworks that guide the development and deployment of new technologies, ensuring that they are aligned with our values and serve the common good. Digital literacy, critical thinking skills, and an understanding of the ethical implications of technology must become essential components of education in the 21st century.

Moreover, we must foster a sense of collective responsibility for the ethical use of technology. Tech companies, policymakers, educators, and individuals all have a role to play in shaping a future where technology empowers ethical action and contributes to a more just, equitable, and sustainable world. This requires ongoing dialogue, collaboration, and a willingness to adapt our ethical frameworks to the ever-evolving technological landscape.